HOLLYWOOD
AT WAR

HOLLYWOOD AT WAR

THE MOTION PICTURE INDUSTRY AND WORLD WAR II

BY CHARNAN SIMON

A First Book
Franklin Watts
New York / Chicago / London / Toronto / Sydney

For Toni and Ed, whose star qualities are obvious

Author's Note: This book was written to commemorate the fiftieth anniversary of the end of World War II, and to celebrate the one hundredth anniversary of the birth of the movies.

Frontispiece: Bob Hope entertains the U.S. troops during World War II.

Cover art by Jane Sterrett

Photographs copyright ©: Archive Photos: pp. 2, 23, 45; The Museum of Modern Art/Film Stills Archive: pp. 8, 18, 20, 43, 55; Wide World Photos: pp. 10, 15, 28, 41, 51; Photofest: pp. 12, 24, 33, 35, 46; Patrick McCarver Collector's Originals, Memphis, Tn.: p. 30; Culver Pictures, Inc.: pp. 36, 49; UPI/Bettmann: pp. 38, 52.

Library of Congress Cataloging-in-Publication Data

Simon, Charnan.
     Hollywood at war : the motion picture industry and World War II / by Charnan Simon
        p. cm. — (A First book)
     Includes bibliographical references (p.) and index.
     ISBN 0-531-20193-7
     1. World War, 1939–1945—Motion pictures and the war—Juvenile literature. 2. Motion pictures—United States—History—20th century—Juvenile literature. 3. Film and the war—Juvenile literature. 4. Propaganda, American—Juvenile literature. [1. World War, 1939–1945. 2. Motion pictures—History.] I. Title. II. Series.
D743.23.S56 1995
791.43'658—dc20   94-27430
                                              CIP
                                              AC

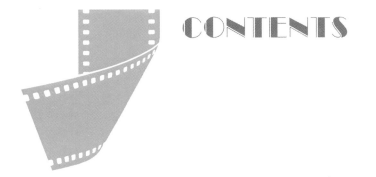

CONTENTS

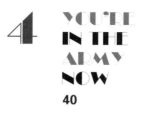
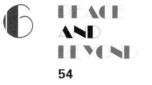

LET'S GO TO THE MOVIES

The year 1939 was a great one for moviemakers in Hollywood, California. While Europe poised uneasily on the brink of war, Hollywood produced two of its biggest blockbusters ever: the musical fantasy *The Wizard of Oz* and the Civil War epic *Gone with the Wind*. Early financial returns from these and other popular films cemented Hollywood's reputation as the world's film capital.

As capitals go, Hollywood wasn't very old. In fact, movies themselves weren't very old in 1939.

The first photographs of motion were shot in the 1870s by a British photographer named Eadweard Muybridge. He set up a row of twelve cameras at a racetrack and shot twelve still pictures of a horse as it galloped past. Put together, the photographs were the first

The Wizard of Oz
by L. Frank Baum

to show movement through pictures. As the story goes, Muybridge shot his historic series to settle a bet about whether or not a galloping horse lifts all four feet off the ground at once!

After Muybridge shot his pictures, the idea of photographing motion attracted a lot of attention. Soon cameras were being invented that would actually record and project moving pictures.

Thomas Edison was the first to show off a commercial motion picture machine when he unveiled his Kinetoscope at the World's Columbian Exposition in Chicago in 1893. People had to look through the Kinetoscope's peephole one at a time to see only about ninety seconds of a lab assistant sneezing, but audiences loved it.

Across the Atlantic Ocean, two French brothers, Louis and Auguste Lumière, were also hard at work. In 1895, they fascinated customers of a Paris café with a moving picture of a train puffing out of a station.

In 1903, a cameraman working for Thomas Edison made a new kind of movie. Instead of just filming events as they happened, Edwin S. Porter actually invented events to be filmed. His first movie, *The Life of an American Fireman*, showed the dramatic rescue of a

Judy Garland as Dorothy poses with the Tin Man, the Scarecrow, the Wizard, and the Cowardly Lion in a promotional shot for the timeless *The Wizard of Oz*.

This is a scene from *The Great Train Robbery*, which established the motion picture as a storytelling medium.

woman and child from a burning building. His next film, *The Great Train Robbery*, was eleven minutes of pure western excitement, and audiences around the country happily paid a nickel to share the thrills.

It was the birth of the motion picture as a major form of art and entertainment. Shown in **vaudeville** theaters and on makeshift screens around the country, silent moving pictures soon became enormously popular.

At first movies were shot mostly on the East Coast. However, by the early 1900s, filmmakers had begun looking westward to southern California. This part of the country offered warm weather and clear skies for year-round shooting, cheap labor costs, and natural scenery that included oceans, deserts, mountains, and lush valleys. And so Hollywood, a dusty little suburb of Los Angeles, became home to the moviemaking industry.

Hollywood flourished. By the time World War I ended in 1918, American movies were the most popular in the world. To audiences everywhere, American movies were synonymous with Hollywood.

Technical developments in filmmaking came quickly. In 1927, a **synchronized sound track** was added to film and the first "talkie," *The Jazz Singer*, was produced. In 1928, Walt Disney came out with *Steamboat Willie*, the first **animated film** with synchronized sound. Three-color Technicolor followed in 1935, with the production of a film called *Becky Sharp*.

It was a glorious time for Hollywood. Film after film experimented with the new technologies of sound and color, delighting audiences around the globe. By 1939,

Built in 1922, the landmark sign in the hills of Hollywood originally read "Hollywoodland." When it was restored in 1978, the last four letters were scrapped.

Hollywood was one of the nation's most successful industries. There were more movie theaters (15,115) than banks (14,952) in America. Fifty million Americans went to the movies weekly to watch the four hundred new films produced annually.

Hollywood was an international force as well. Some 80 percent of all the movies seen in the world came out of film canisters shot in Hollywood. The movie moguls of Hollywood earned more than a third of their income from foreign distribution.

But the world was not a stable place in 1939. In Europe, **Fascist dictators** Adolf Hitler and Benito Mussolini had been rising to frightening power in Germany and Italy. In the Pacific, Japan was aggressively trying to bring all of eastern Asia under its control.

On September 1, 1939, the storm clouds that had been gathering over Europe finally broke when Germany invaded Poland. World War II had officially begun. What would happen to Hollywood movies—and to Hollywood profits—now?

RUMBLINGS OF WAR

Filmmaking in Hollywood didn't change dramatically after the invasion of Poland. The industry was well regulated and required more than the rumblings of war in faraway Europe to shake it.

A powerful studio system dominated the workings of Hollywood in 1939. The "Big Eight" studios—M-G-M, Paramount, Universal, Warner Brothers, 20th-Century Fox, RKO, Columbia, and United Artists—controlled virtually every aspect of Hollywood moviemaking. The studios owned the movie stars' time, the moviemaking equipment, the distribution rights, and even the theaters where their movies were shown. The men who ran these studios hobnobbed with presidents and earned enormous salaries. M-G-M's head, Louis B. Mayer, was the highest paid man in the United States from 1939 to 1950.

During Hollywood's prewar heyday, going to the movies was a weekly ritual. Here, the line for the New York City premiere of *Gone with the Wind* stretches far beyond the box office.

Rich and powerful as they were, most studio heads wanted nothing to do with international politics. They carefully avoided taking a stand on **fascism** as Hitler and Mussolini rose to power in the early 1930s.

There were several reasons for this "hands-off" attitude. First, Hollywood filmmakers had a traditional American distrust of getting involved in foreign problems; Hitler and Mussolini were European, not American, headaches. At that time, too, the most vocal anti-Fascist group in America was the Communist party, never a very popular group in mainstream America. Finally, there was the uncomfortable fact that Hollywood, like much of America in the 1930s, was itself somewhat anti-Semitic. Jewish people were excluded from many neighborhoods and clubs, and a quota system limited the number of Jews at certain colleges and businesses. Hollywood may not have embraced Hitler's campaign of hatred against the Jewish race, but as a community, it didn't speak out against the campaign, either.

In part, this was because the movie studios, in business to make money, had their profits to protect. With a large chunk of those profits coming from foreign distribution, studio heads didn't want to offend European audiences, Fascist or anti-Fascist. The official reason for Hollywood staying out of the war in Europe was the Hollywood Production Code. This code, established in 1934 by the motion picture industry, outlined what was right and proper to appear in films. It was Hollywood's way of censoring itself, to avoid offending the majority of the movie-watching public.

The Production Code advised filmmakers to make it clear that crime didn't pay, marriage was sacred, Christianity was the true religion, and that "the just rights, history, and feeling of any nation are entitled to consideration and respectful treatment." It was this last clause, and a $25,000 fine for noncompliance, that discouraged filmmakers from producing films that were blatantly anti-Fascist, or that urged American involvement in Europe's war.

Most studio heads willingly abided by the Production Code. As Louis B. Mayer of M-G-M explained, "This is a large corporation. I'm responsible for stockholders. We have theaters all over the world, including Berlin. We don't make hate pictures. We don't hate anyone. We're not at war." M-G-M was so determined to avoid offending Germany that they removed all the Jewish-sounding names from the credits of films headed for Berlin.

Louis Mayer, like nearly all the major studio heads, was Jewish. He and others defended their conciliatory attitude toward Hitler by arguing that antagonizing the Führer would only make things worse for their fellow Jews in Europe. Critics of this point of view scoffed that the studios just didn't want to lose money by making Hitler mad enough to ban their films.

Warner Brothers was an exception. Jack Warner despised Hitler, and he didn't mind making movies that said so. As a studio, Warner Brothers had always had a reputation for making films with a social message, and that message was now clearly anti-Fascist. There was a personal reason for Jack Warner's bias, too. In 1936, the

Louis B. Mayer (left) and Jack Warner (right)

studio's Berlin representative, Joe Kaufman, was beaten and kicked to death by Nazi thugs. Warner Brothers immediately closed their Berlin office. Three years later, they came out with the first openly anti-Fascist Hollywood film, *Confessions of a Nazi Spy*. Its release brought an official complaint from the German government and death threats to Jack Warner.

By late 1939, the rest of Hollywood was beginning to become more war conscious. The rise of fascism had brought some of Europe's best film talents, such as Billy Wilder, Luis Buñuel, and Jean Renoir, to seek refuge in Hollywood. One Berlin-born actress named Marlene Dietrich received a request from Hitler to make movies for the Nazis, which she refused. When she became an American citizen in 1939, Hitler denounced her for betraying "the Fatherland."

The German director Fritz Lang probably had the most dramatic escape story. Adolf Hitler was such a fan of Lang's film *Metropolis* that he had his Minister of **Propaganda** and Public Enlightenment, Joseph Goebbels, ask Lang to manage all Nazi film production. Lang, who was part Jewish, didn't trust the offer and within twenty-four hours had fled Berlin under an assumed name.

When war looked imminent after the signing of the Hitler-Stalin pact on August 23, 1939, Hollywood realized how many of its stars were in Europe. Hollywood rushed to bring home popular stars such as Tyrone Power, Charles Boyer, Robert Montgomery, Maureen O'Sullivan, and Bob Hope.

When Britain and France officially declared war, Hollywood was in a quandary. How could the studios make movies that sympathized with the troubles of their British, Polish, and French audiences, without offending their German and Italian fans?

For example, Charlie Chaplin's *The Great Dictator* was a biting anti-Fascist **satire** in which Chaplin played

both a humble Jewish barber and a villain who looked suspiciously like Adolf Hitler. The great silent film star felt strongly enough about fascism that for the first time ever, he spoke comprehensible words on the screen. At the movie's end, Chaplin pleaded for international peace and brotherhood: "The clouds are lifting! The sun is breaking through!" During filming in 1939, Chaplin worried that its anti-Nazi theme might get him in trouble with the censors. When the film was released a year later, Chaplin had a different worry—that audiences might be offended by his slapstick treatment of such a deadly serious subject.

The war was hard for Hollywood in other ways, too. Once war was declared, fewer Europeans were watching movies. Many were fighting, of course, and **blackout laws**, **curfews**, and other wartime rules meant that many more were just staying home. Then there were the practical problems of getting the films to Europe. With submarines patrolling undersea and bombers flying overhead, transporting movies across the Atlantic was both difficult and dangerous.

Money continued to be a problem for Hollywood. Countries at war need money to build tanks, buy ammunition, and feed soldiers. Even friendly countries such as

Charlie Chaplin wrote, directed, and acted in nearly all his films. In *The Great Dictator*, he played a Hitler-like tyrant who wanted to control the world.

France and Britain didn't like Hollywood taking home all those movie profits. Naturally, unfriendly nations like Germany and Italy didn't appreciate Hollywood taking profits, either.

When Italy and Germany eventually banned American movies altogether, the Hollywood studios were able to produce films that openly supported France and Britain and opposed fascism. Still, even as late as 1941, many Americans wanted to stay out of the war in Europe. Those who thought Europeans should settle their own conflicts were called isolationists; those who thought the United States should join the fight against the Nazi threat were called interventionists.

Hollywood still wasn't completely pro-war. Two of its biggest hits of 1941—*Citizen Kane*, the life story of an ambitious newspaperman, and *How Green Was My Valley*, the story of a close-knit coal-mining family from Wales—were unrelated to the European conflict. Other important films clearly did promote the war. Serious movies such as *A Yank in the RAF*, *Flight Command*, and *Dive Bomber* and comedies such as *Caught in the Draft* and *Buck Privates* were quickly dubbed "preparedness pix" for their efforts to prepare American audiences for war.

Probably the two most famous "preparedness pix" were *Sergeant York* and *Mrs. Miniver*. In *Sergeant York*, Oscar-winning Gary Cooper played a World War I sergeant who became a hero after overcoming his religious objection to war. Some complained that *Sergeant York* encouraged the American public to overcome their objec-

In *A Yank in the RAF,* Tyrone Power plays an American pilot who joins the British Royal Air Force. This is one of the actor's studio shots.

tions to war. The Academy Award-winning *Mrs. Miniver* took a different approach, with Scottish actress Greer Garson as a heroic British wife and mother coping on the home front. Self-sacrificing and ever hopeful, Garson inspired tremendous support for the British when the movie was made in 1941. Britain's Queen Mother commented, "It was such a morale booster for us when we most needed it. We had no idea that we were quite so brave and were very pleased to be told that we were so heroic."

Not everyone was so very pleased. On September 23, 1941, a congressional subcommittee met to discuss "Moving Pictures Screen and Radio Propaganda." Isolationist congressmen accused Hollywood of turning theaters into "daily and nightly mass meetings for war," and warned that the studios wanted "to rouse war fever in America and plunge the nation to her destruction."

All discussion of whether or not Hollywood ought to support the war ended on December 7, 1941. On that historic date, the Japanese staged a surprise bomb attack on U.S. naval bases at Pearl Harbor in Hawaii. Like it or not, America was at war.

In *Mrs. Miniver*, Greer Garson played a courageous mother in wartime Britain. The film drew support for the war on both sides of the Atlantic.

HOLLYWOOD MOBILIZES

After the bombing of Pearl Harbor, Hollywood lost no time joining the war effort. All the studios began cranking out pro-war, anti-enemy movies such as *Wings over the Pacific*, *V for Victory*, *Yellow Peril*, *Spy Smashers*, and *Secret Agent of Japan*.

This time Washington didn't object. Once the country was officially at war, the government wanted to encourage all Americans to support the fighting with their hearts and souls. In the coming years, Americans would be asked to give up many things for the war effort. Automobiles, appliances, rubber and leather goods, and even food would be severely **rationed**. People would be urged to raise their own vegetables in backyard **Victory Gardens**, collect scrap iron and newspapers, work long hours in war-goods factories and shipyards, and sacrifice beloved husbands, sons, brothers, and fathers as wartime casualties.

The national government in Washington realized how useful Hollywood could be in mobilizing the home front. After all, in 1941, some ninety million Americans relaxed at their neighborhood cinema every week. Propaganda films designed to help the war effort would go a long way toward making the average American believe that the enemy was evil, home was worth protecting, and all the danger and difficulties of war were justified. The government quickly proclaimed movies an "essential industry," much like coal and steel production, shipbuilding, and food processing. Movies weren't exactly a line of defense, but they could certainly be the nation's cheerleader.

President Franklin D. Roosevelt explained exactly what he meant in his State of the Union address to Congress in January 1942. There were six areas around which he felt film propaganda should be based: the issues of war (why we are fighting), the nature of the enemy, the united nations (our **allies** in arms), the production front, the home front, and the fighting forces.

Realizing that war movies could be popular and profitable, Hollywood was only too happy to oblige. Early war movies were mostly romanticized. Instead of showing the grim reality of life on the front, films such as *Wake Island* and *Guadalcanal Diary* tried to raise morale and encourage enthusiasm for the war. In 1943, possibly the best war romance ever made, *Casablanca* won an Academy Award for best picture.

Propaganda films portrayed "the nature of the enemy" and didn't pretend to give America's enemies any individuality or humanity. The films were designed to show the enemy's warped values and how those values threatened the American way of life. "They" were the bad guys; "we" were the good guys.

Movies such as *Suspicion*, *Five Graves to Cairo* by Austrian refugee Billy Wilder, and *The Hitler Gang* portrayed German officers as cold, cruel, and sophisticated, and German foot soldiers as cold, cruel, and thick-headed. In *Tomorrow, the World*, even Nazi children were portrayed as brainwashed little robots that threatened America.

One movie that broke the mold was the 1942 anti-Nazi parody *To Be or Not to Be*. Starring Jack Benny and Carole Lombard, the film pitted a German theatrical company against the Nazis. The humor was sharp and satiric and the realism was unsettling.

America's Japanese enemies were often shown to be even more evil than the Germans. In movie after

On December 8, 1941, President Franklin D. Roosevelt asks Congress for an immediate declaration of war. In his State of the Union address a month later, the president spoke about the film industry's role in the war effort.

WARNER BROS. PICTURES, INC. PRESENTS

Humphrey
BOGART
Ingrid
BERGMAN
Paul
HENREID

IN

"CASABLANCA"

A HAL B. WALLIS PRODUCTION
A WARNER BROS · FIRST NATIONAL PICTURE

movie, Japanese forces bombed Red Cross hospitals and tortured American soldiers. They showed no remorse for their evil acts and acted apparently without conscience. Films such as *Bataan* and *Objective Burma* left no doubt in audiences' minds that the Japanese were an enemy well worth fighting.

Propaganda movies were also made to gain sympathy and support for U.S. allies abroad. Movies such as *White Cliffs of Dover*, *This Land Is Mine*, *Edge of Darkness*, and *Mission to Moscow* called attention to the difficult living conditions and admirable courage of the citizens of Britain, France, Norway, and Russia. These movies **stereotyped** the Allied countries as much as they did the enemy. In these films, the Allied people were shown to be good, honorable, and brave; any normal human flaws might have made them seem less worthy of American sacrifices and assistance.

Other movies were made to boost morale (and production) at home. In these films plucky, honest, and generous Americans on the home front hid their sorrow, showed their courage, and never lost their Yankee ingenuity and sense of humor. *The More the Merrier* made light of wartime shortages. *Tender Comrades* showed

In 1943, superb performances from Humphrey Bogart and Ingrid Bergman made *Casablanca* the ultimate wartime romance picture.

how factory-worker wives kept their hearts pure and their spirits high while their husbands were fighting—and dying—on the battlefields. The family drama *Since You Went Away* was probably the ultimate home-front war movie. As its introductory title proclaimed: "This is the story of an unconquerable fortress, the American home, 1943."

As the war progressed, films about U.S. fighting forces became less romantic and more grimly realistic. *A Walk in the Sun* gave a minute-by-minute account of a day in the life of an army platoon in Italy. *The Purple Heart* was a fictional account of eight American airmen who were shot down over Tokyo, tortured, and finally executed. Although the film was made in 1944, it wasn't released until after the war, when the U.S. government officially acknowledged that the Japanese had in fact tortured American prisoners. The romantic *So Proudly We Hail* was one of the few movies that paid tribute to the combat nurses who served on the front lines. Arguably the best of the later war films was *The Story of G.I. Joe*, made in 1945. Based on the writings of wartime correspondent Ernie Pyle, this film had an authenticity that other combat movies lacked.

Through all its efforts to boost the war, Hollywood had help from the U.S. government. Early in 1942, Washington established the **Office of War Information** (OWI) to advise Hollywood on wartime film production. The OWI sat in on movie planning sessions, provided technical advice on combat and other scenes, reviewed screenplays, and sometimes even wrote key pieces of

This still from *The Purple Heart* is
Hollywood's idea of a Japanese prison.
Eight actors (two are not shown here) play
American airmen captured by the Japanese
and put on trial for war crimes.

dialogue. Its official function was to make every Hollywood producer keep in mind one basic question: "Will this picture help win the war?"

Of course, not all movies were war propaganda. Soldiers and civilians needed to be entertained as well as instructed, and westerns, romances, comedies, mysteries, dramas, and adventures flourished during the war. Especially popular were films about animals and children, which were set far from the ravages of war. *Lassie Come Home*, *National Velvet*, *My Friend Flicka*, *The Yearling*, and *The Red Pony* all portrayed simpler times and places where children and their lovable animal friends romped in peace and safety. When Walt Disney Studio wasn't making educational films for the U.S. government, it was turning out enormously popular animated films of the early 1940s such as *Fantasia*, *Dumbo*, and *Bambi*.

For pure escapism, nothing could beat a musical comedy. Some musicals—*This Is the Army*, *Hollywood Canteen*, *Yankee Doodle Dandy*, and *Anchors Aweigh*—were flag-waving morale boosters. Others—Judy Garland's *Meet Me in St. Louis*, Rita Hayworth's *Cover Girl*, and Busby Berkeley's *The Gang's All Here*—just as deliberately avoided any mention of war or hard times.

The undisputed queen of the wartime musical was the blond-haired actress Betty Grable. Calling herself "strictly the **enlisted man**'s girl," Grable appeared in more than a dozen musicals between 1941 and 1945 and was the top box-office draw in 1943. She was also arguably the **GI**'s favorite pinup girl—the argument coming from those soldiers who preferred Rita Hayworth's

In *Fantasia*, Disney mixed animation with classical music. Mickey Mouse makes a famous cameo appearance in this comedic segment set to "The Sorcerer's Apprentice."

black satin shimmering to Betty Grable's sparkle and charm!

Hollywood was only too happy to make movies starring Betty Grable, Rita Hayworth, and other stars favored by U.S. servicemen. During the war years, the U.S. government was one of the largest theater operators in the world, setting up some six hundred new theaters in military camps in the United States and abroad. It made sense for Hollywood to aim to please its military audiences.

Although filmmaking had been declared an essential industry, Hollywood had to make wartime sacrifices like the rest of the nation. Because film was made of cellulose, which was also used to make explosives, 25 percent less film was available to make movies. Less film meant fewer takes, so actors had to rehearse more to get it right the first time. Materials for sets, props, and costumes were also in short supply. Everything that could be reused was. Sugar rationing put an end to the spun-sugar windows that broke easily during staged fights. Lack of balsa wood from the Philippines, which was under fierce fighting at the time, meant no more lightweight chairs to break over heads.

The wartime appearances of Hollywood stars helped to keep up the spirits of those in the military. Here, the popular Betty Grable autographs her famous pinup picture for some fans in uniform.

19 CALIFORNIA 42
7W 45 54
PLEASE DRIVE CAREFULLY
MY BUMPERS ARE ON THE SCRAP HEAP

Some interesting innovations came out of the shortages. Studios that couldn't build elaborate sets anymore began experimenting with shooting their films in the real world. Alfred Hitchcock's 1943 film, *Shadow of a Doubt*, about a psychopathic killer in small-town America, was the first film shot entirely on location.

There were other changes in Hollywood. Restaurants and nightclubs shut down. Yachts were turned over to the Navy and Coast Guard. Polo ponies were given to West Point. Swimming pool owners were ordered to keep their pools filled to prevent water shortages in the event of a Japanese attack.

One Hollywood shortage that couldn't be easily made up was the lack of Japanese actors. After the bombing of Pearl Harbor, many white Americans began to suspect unfairly that their Japanese neighbors were enemies. In February 1942, 112,000 Japanese Americans were sent from their homes on the West Coast to "relocation camps," where they were imprisoned for the remainder of the war. Without Japanese actors in Hollywood, the studios had to rely on Korean and Chinese actors to play Japanese villains in their war propaganda movies. It was a boon to several previously unknown Asian actors, but a blemish on America's human-rights record.

Celebrities were often enlisted to help publicize salvage drives. Rita Hayworth does her part.

YOU'RE IN THE ARMY NOW

Commercial movies were not Hollywood's only contribution to World War II. Actors, directors, producers, writers, and technicians served the war effort in many other valuable ways, such as joining the armed forces. Major stars such as Jimmy Stewart, Robert Montgomery, William Holden, British actor David Niven, and Tyrone Power enlisted and served honorably on the front. Others, like a young cavalry reservist named Ronald Reagan, enlisted but were eventually sent back to Hollywood to make training films.

The studios didn't want their actors to enlist, preferring them to stay in Hollywood to make movies and profits. Studio heads used their clout to keep their stars out of the armed forces and were frequently successful. When they failed, each celebrity's call to duty was turned into a major publicity event.

Movie actor Jimmy Stewart put aside his Hollywood career and joined the ranks of the U.S. armed forces. Major Stewart drives a bomber crew to its waiting plane at a base in England.

The American public itself had mixed feelings about movie stars going to war. On the one hand, no one wanted a favorite celebrity killed in battle. On the other hand, the average American resented the ease with which Hollywood personnel seemed to avoid active duty.

In general, the government in Washington agreed with the studios that movie stars were more valuable in Hollywood than on the front. The government encouraged celebrities to serve the war effort by making propaganda films, entertaining the troops, and selling **war bonds**.

By October 1942, 12 percent of Hollywood personnel—some 2,700 movie people—had joined the armed forces. Many of those who put on uniforms actually fought. Jimmy Stewart became a bomber pilot and eventually a lieutenant colonel in the Army. Robert Montgomery commanded a Navy destroyer at the invasion of Normandy. Tyrone Power became a transport pilot in the South Pacific.

Many Hollywood directors helped the war effort by making movies. Frank Capra, whose well-known movies include *Arsenic and Old Lace* and *It's a Wonderful Life*, became a major in the 834th Photo Signal Detachment. His assignment, as explained by chief of staff General George Marshall, was to make a series of documentaries "that will explain to our boys in the Army *why* we are fighting." The result was Capra's *Why We Fight* series, seven one-hour documentaries on the causes and origins of World War II.

Darryl Zanuck, head of 20th-Century Fox, was com-

**Third in the "Why We Fight" series, *Divide and Conquer*
includes this scene from a captured German film of Hitler
reviewing his troops after they had crushed France.**

missioned as a colonel in the Army Signal Corps. Before
he left Hollywood, he fired off a series of patriotic films
such as *To the Shores of Tripoli* and *Tonight We Raid
Calais*. Once in the army, Zanuck made numerous train-

ing films, with such exciting titles as *Military Courtesy and Customs of the Service* and *The 37-mm Anti-Aircraft Gun Battery—Care After Firings*.

Director John Ford rose to the ranks of rear admiral in the Navy and was chief of the Field Photographic Branch of the **OSS** (Office of Strategic Services). Ford made a number of documentaries, including his most famous, *The Battle of Midway*. The film was shot during an actual attack, and Ford received not an Academy Award, but a Purple Heart for the wound he received during filming.

The armed forces worked hand in hand with Hollywood in making wartime documentaries. In 1942, Hollywood owned 80 percent of the world's sound cameras. The armed forces needed some of these cameras—and the technicians who operated them—to make their own training, orientation, and propaganda films. In one of the most extensive collaborations, the Army Air Corps took over the commercial Hal Roach studio and turned it into "Fort Roach." Instead of shooting feature films, the First Motion Picture Unit trained combat camera units, produced documentaries and combat film newsreels for commercial theaters, and even made films that simulated flight over bomb targets for pilots to see what the targets looked like from the air.

U.S. airplanes bomb a Japanese cruiser in this still from *The Battle of Midway*.

Wartime Disney cartoons often emphasized patriotic themes. In *Der Fuehrer's Face*, Donald Duck kisses a Statue of Liberty miniature and croons, "Am I glad to be a citizen of the United States of America."

At the government's request, filmmakers also turned out political propaganda. The Office of War Information used Hollywood studios to make pro-democracy, anti-Fascist documentaries such as *The American Scene*. Hitler himself had long been using American films for his own purposes. By re-editing gangster films, the Nazis could show America as a land of tommy guns and city slums, where the bad guys always won.

A number of films were made to be shown in France and other occupied countries after the Allies liberated them from the Nazis. Some of these films were meant to make the occupied countries see how the rest of the world admired them. Others were designed to help war-torn countries catch up on world events they had missed during the fighting.

Hollywood found itself helping out in other, unexpected ways. Southern California was home to two-thirds of the nation's major aircraft plants. After the bombing of Pearl Harbor everyone worried about possible Japanese attacks. Since Walt Disney's studios were next door to the Lockheed aircraft plant, an Army guard unit moved in with Mickey Mouse and Donald Duck, to better protect the aircraft plant. The nearby Douglas aircraft plant was so concerned about security, they hired Warner Brothers' special effects technicians to camouflage their buildings. Warners did such a good job, Lockheed asked them to do the same for their plant!

CANTEENS, CARAVANS, AND KISSES

The Hollywood personnel who didn't enlist spent their war years entertaining or raising money for the troops. Since almost all the servicemen bound for the Pacific shipped out of nearby Los Angeles, Hollywood was an ideal place for entertaining troops. The Hollywood Canteen was formed as a place where servicemen and stars could socialize and relax. The president of the Canteen, movie star Bette Davis, rounded up virtually all the stars left in Hollywood to perform, serve cookies, wash dishes, and take turns on the dance floor with nervous young sailors and soldiers.

Other celebrities spent their war years touring munitions plants, hospitals, training camps, and military bases in the United States and abroad. From Hawaii to the South Pacific, from Europe to the Middle East, these

Marlene Dietrich contributed much of her time to the war effort. Here, the actress serves a coastguardsman a cup of coffee at the opening of the Hollywood Canteen.

actors and actresses logged thousands of miles singing, dancing, and telling jokes to homesick people in the service all over the world.

Comedian Bob Hope was the undisputed king of the traveling celebrities and performed almost nonstop throughout the war. During one three-month period in 1943, he put on more than 250 shows!

Hollywood stars also put their talents to good use selling war bonds, which were used to pay for America's war effort. When actress Hedy Lamarr offered to kiss any man who bought $25,000 worth of bonds, she sold $17 million in a single day. Lana Turner charged $50,000 per kiss—and she had no trouble collecting. Dorothy Lamour was probably the most successful saleswoman. Dubbed the "Sweetheart of the Treasury," Lamour once sold $30 million of bonds in four days. By the war's end she had collected more than $350 million—with and without kisses.

There were wartime tragedies even selling war bonds. Clark Gable won millions of women's hearts as the dashing Rhett Butler in *Gone with the Wind*. In 1942, he became the head of the Hollywood Victory Committee and helped organize a war bond-selling tour for his wife Carole Lombard. Lombard, who had recently starred in *To Be or Not to Be,* sold more than $2 million in less than two weeks. On the return trip to Hollywood, Lombard's plane crashed, killing the thirty-four-year-old actress. While his legion of fans mourned with him, the devastated Gable joined the army, where he served as an aerial gunner.

The Victory Caravans offered another way for Holly-

Film actress Dorothy Lamour, known affection-
ately as the "Sweetheart of the Treasury,"
posts an advertisement for war bonds.

Clark Gable and Carole Lombard arrive
at a war-relief fund-raiser in Hollywood.

wood celebrities to serve the war effort. Loaded with actors, actresses, musicians, and technicians, these star-studded trains crisscrossed the country selling war bonds. Day after day, stars such as Bing Crosby, Groucho Marx, Greer Garson, Claudette Colbert, and Cary Grant marched in parades, gave interviews, attended dinners, and put on three- to four-hour evening shows to raise money. One night in Chicago, they netted more than $90,000 in a single performance.

Bing Crosby and Bob Hope organized golf benefits. Jimmy Cagney, star of *Yankee Doodle Dandy*, marched in countless parades. Marlene Dietrich joked that she had "joined the army," as she performed in **USO** (United Service Organization) shows for GIs around the country. Dozens of other actors and actresses auctioned off articles of clothing and jewelry as bonuses for buying war bonds. Even Mickey Mouse and Donald Duck did animated shorts, encouraging audiences to grow Victory Gardens. They may not have been in uniform, but Hollywood celebrities did their best to serve the war effort.

Although celebrities often supported the war out of honest patriotic feelings, sometimes they just did what their studios told them to do. While the studio heads may have had patriotic motivations, it never hurt a studio's reputation when its stars were photographed pouring coffee at the Hollywood Canteen or crawling into a bunk on the Victory Caravan. America's twelve million servicemen and servicewomen were now Hollywood's biggest—and most captive—audience, and it was only fair that the studios give something in return for the tremendous profits they were reaping from the war.

PEACE AND BEYOND

On May 8, 1945, Germany surrendered to the Allied forces, ending the war in Europe. On September 2, 1945, Japan signed the surrender papers that concluded the war in the Pacific. World War II was over.

After the war Hollywood, like the rest of America, returned to civilian life. Between December 1941 and December 1945, the major studios had released 1,321 films. In three out of every ten of these films, the main story line involved the war. While war films would be made for years to come, they would never again be as popular as they had been during the actual war years. Films now focused on homecomings and building new lives.

Hollywood's view of those new lives was somewhat

The Best Years of Our Lives debuted soon after the end of World War II. Audiences trying to put their lives together again after the war found the film timely and poignant. It won seven Academy Awards.

mixed. The 1946 film *The Best Years of Our Lives* looked at the fears and anxieties of three soldiers returning home from the war. For these three soldiers, and perhaps for millions like them, the best years of their lives were not the postwar years, but the years already spent on the bloody battlefields of World War II. The sober film must have struck a chord with the American public because it swept the Academy Awards in 1946.

Three years later, Hollywood was looking at returning soldiers with a jauntier eye. The musical comedy *On the Town* was a masterpiece of artistic and musical innovation. It put aside the realism of returning to civilian life, and audiences loved the tap-dancing magic of this fairy-tale romance.

And so Hollywood went on making movies. Some directors and producers, shaped by their experiences in World War II, turned out socially relevant films with serious, thought-provoking messages. Others, just as shaped by their wartime experiences, put aside the horrors of war and returned to familiar genres with lighthearted, escapist themes.

The postwar years brought many changes to Hollywood. The studio system began to break apart and open the way for independent producers and smaller studios. European art films grew in popularity and competed with more conservative Hollywood offerings. Television was invented, encouraging moviegoers to stay home for evening entertainment.

By the 1950s, the old Hollywood of stars and studios was gone. But for a few brief years during World War II, Hollywood had pooled its people and its resources to support the nation's war effort with energy, enthusiasm, and an enormous amount of talent.

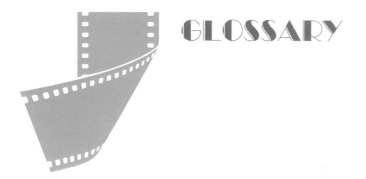

GLOSSARY

Allies — People, groups, or countries that work together to help each other. During World War II, the Allied countries, led by the United States, Britain, and the U.S.S.R., united against Germany and its allies.

Animated films — A motion picture made from a series of drawings, each slightly different from the one before it. When the drawings are projected in rapid motion, the figures in the drawings appear to move.

Blackout laws — A wartime regulation that required citizens to turn out lights after dark to make it harder for enemy bombers to spot them as targets during air raids.

Curfews — A time, frequently sunset, after which citizens have to be off the streets and in their homes.

Dictator — A person who rules absolutely, often using

power unfairly and without getting approval from citizens.

Enlisted man — A man who signs up for service in the army or another branch of the armed forces.

Fascism; Fascist — A method of government with an absolute dictator, strong military, great emphasis on nationalism, and little or no individual freedom for citizens; a person who advocates fascism.

GI — The letters themselves stand for "government issue," but the term is understood to mean any member or former member of any of the U.S. armed forces.

OSS (Office of Strategic Services) — A secret intelligence agency of the U.S. government during World War II.

OWI (Office of War Information) — A U.S. government agency established to encourage public support for World War II.

Propaganda — Information or ideas spread by a person or group of persons that is meant to try to change the way other people think. Propaganda often gives only one side of the story and may not be completely true.

Ration — To limit a person's supply of a good. In times of shortages, goods are rationed to make them last longer.

Satire — Sarcasm or wit used to make fun of a person, custom, belief, or idea.

Stereotype — To hold an overly simplified image or idea about a person or group that doesn't allow for individual judgments.

Synchronized sound track — A recording of words and music (made along one edge of a motion picture film) that is designed to match exactly the film's action.

USO (United Service Organization) — A civilian non-profit organization founded in 1941 to serve the members of the U.S. armed forces and their families.

Vaudeville — A type of live theatrical entertainment that includes a variety of unrelated acts, such as singing, dancing, acrobatic shows, comedy routines, and trained animal performances.

Victory Gardens — Vegetable gardens that Americans were urged to grow so that more commercially grown food could be sent to the troops. They were so named because the gardeners were doing their part for victory in the war.

War bonds — Certificates bought from the government to help fund a war effort. After a certain amount of time, the buyer redeems the bond and the government gives back the purchase price of the bond, plus interest payments.

FOR FURTHER READING

Black, Wallace B., and Jean F. Blashfield. *America Prepares for War*. New York: Macmillan Children's Group, 1991.

Dowd, Ned. *That's a Wrap: How Movies Are Made*. New York: Simon and Schuster, 1991.

Hoopes, Roy. *When the Stars Went to War: Hollywood and World War II*. New York: Random House, 1995.

Killingray, David, and Malcolm Yapp. *Hollywood*. San Diego: Greenhaven, 1980.

Meyer, Nicholas E. *Magic in the Dark: A Young Viewer's History of the Movies*. New York: Facts on File, 1985.

Whitman, Sylvia. *V Is for Victory: The American Homefront During World War II*. Minneapolis: Lerner Publications, 1992.

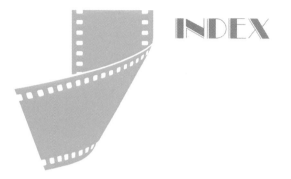

INDEX

ABOUT THE AUTHOR

Charnan Simon began her publishing career at Little, Brown and Company. After that, she spent five busy years as an editor of *Cricket* magazine, where she read hundreds of great children's books and met many talented writers and artists. All of this was a tremendous help when she started writing her own books for young readers. Ms. Simon lives in Madison, Wisconsin, with her husband Tom, her two daughters, Ariel and Hana, and her dog, Sam. She especially likes reading—and writing—history, biography, and fiction of all sorts. Her favorite Hollywood films are *The Music Man*, *Singing in the Rain*, and *The Shop Around the Corner*.